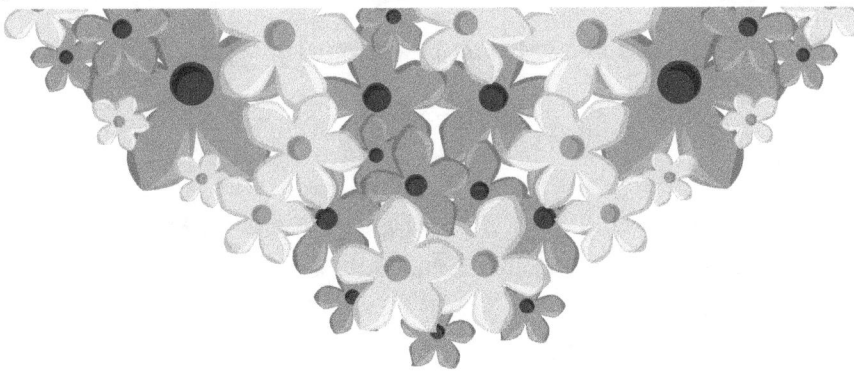

The Life Graduate Publishing Group

No part of this book may be scanned, reproduced or distributed in any printed or electronic form without the prior permission of the author or publisher.
Copyright - The Life Graduate Publishing Group 2020 - All Rights Reserved

We love to receive reviews from our customers. If you had the opportunity to provide a review we would greatly appreciate it. Thank you!

I Wrote This Book For You Nanny!
Mother's Day

← This is me!

Created By:

Year:

My Age: ____ yrs

We celebrate Mother's Day on..

MONTH _____

DAY _____

I love the smell of flowers!!

Happy Mother's Day Nanny. I wrote this book for you because......

_____

_____

_____

_____

This is a drawing of you and I on Mother's Day.

Nanny and I

These are 3 things you do that are kind.

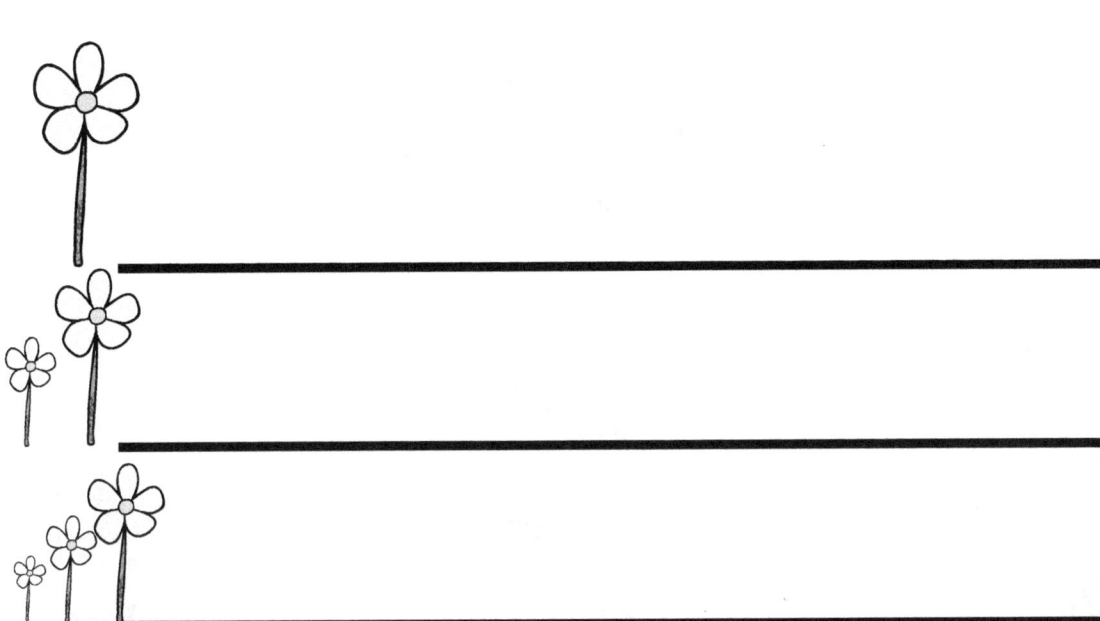

I LOVE IT WHEN YOU...

This is somewhere I love to visit with you.

I would like to say thank you for helping me to....

8

This is a drawing of you →

You like to relax by doing this..

RELAX

Nanny, I would like you to teach me how to do this...

If I could take you anywhere in the whole wide-world on Mother's Day it would be..

MOTHER'S DAY BOARDING PASS　　　SEAT: **1A**

DEPARTING LOCATION

ARRIVING LOCATION

Nanny, you make me laugh when..

If I created a mother's day t-shirt for you, it would look like this...

You can do this better than anyone else!

Your favorite treat to eat is...

I hope that one day we can do this together..

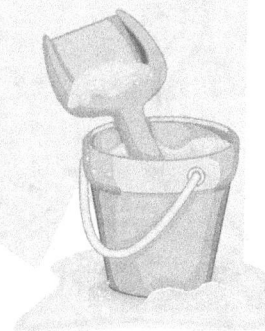

You cook the best......

I colored in this flower for you!

These are 3 words that best describe you!

1. _____

2. _____

3. _____

SPECIAL MOMENTS or MEMORIES

Add other special photo's or drawings here ↙

SPECIAL MOMENTS or MEMORIES

Add other special photo's or drawings here

SPECIAL MOMENTS or MEMORIES

Add other special photo's or drawings here

SPECIAL MOMENTS or MEMORIES

Add other special photo's or drawings here ↙

WISHING YOU A WONDERFUL MOTHER'S DAY

Add your kisses and hugs here!

THIS HAS BEEN MY SPECIAL MOTHER'S DAY GIFT THAT I HAVE CREATED FOR YOU.
I HOPE YOU LIKE IT!

A sample of other books created by
The Life Graduate Publishing Group

www.thelifegraduate.com/bookstore

www.ingramcontent.com/pod-product-compliance
Lightning Source LLC
LaVergne TN
LVHW081525060526
838200LV00044B/2009